Sue Cleaver

Susan Cleaver (born 2 September 1963) is an English actress, best known for her role as Eileen Grimshaw on the ITV soap opera Coronation Street, a character she has portrayed since 2000.

Early and Personal Life

Cleaver was born in Barnet, Hertfordshire, and was adopted as a child. In her twenties, she reconnected with her birth mother and discovered two half-sisters, actresses Emma and Kate Harbour. She was previously married to James Quinn, with whom she has a son, Elliot, born in 1998. Later, she married lighting technician Brian Owen, whom she met on the set of Coronation Street. In 2010, she faced a drink-driving charge, resulting in a 17-month driving ban and a £1,000 fine.

Career

Susan Cleaver trained at the Manchester Metropolitan School of Theatre, beginning her acting career with a small role in A Touch of Frost. She gained recognition in Band of Gold and starred in the film Girls' Night alongside Julie Walters and Brenda Blethyn. Her television credits expanded with roles such as Duty Sgt. Standish in The Cops and Glenda in Victoria Wood's comedy series dinnerladies. She appeared as PC Sylvia Holland in the miniseries This Is Personal: The Hunt for the Yorkshire Ripper and had a minor role in The Man Who Cried with Johnny Depp and Cate Blanchett.

In 2000, Cleaver joined Coronation Street as Eileen Grimshaw, earning acclaim for her portrayal of Eileen, a mother navigating her son Todd's journey of self-acceptance. Alongside acting, she served as an agony aunt on This Morning, covering for Denise Robertson until 2016, and trained as a psychotherapist.

In 2022, Cleaver was a contestant on I'm a Celebrity...Get Me Out of Here!, placing ninth after 16 days. She also appeared on the ITV show Loose Women, initially as a guest in 2023 and later as a regular panelist in 2024. Additionally, in 2024, she published her first book, A Work In Progress, with Bloomsbury.

Charity Work

Cleaver is an active patron of Prevent Breast Cancer and When You Wish Upon a Star, demonstrating her commitment to health and child welfare causes.

Awards and Nominations

Throughout her career, Cleaver has received numerous nominations and awards, including a Best Actress nomination at the 2006 British Soap Awards and a win for Favourite Female Soap Star at the 2007 TV Now Awards. She was also nominated for Best On-Screen Partnership at the 2007 British Soap Awards alongside Ryan Thomas.

Filmography Highlights

A Touch of Frost (1994) as Patten's Receptionist
Band of Gold (1995) as Jan
The Cops (1998) as Duty Sgt. Standish
dinnerladies (1999–2000) as Glenda
Coronation Street (2000–present) as Eileen Grimshaw
I'm a Celebrity...Get Me Out of Here! (2022) as Herself
Loose Women (2010, 2015, 2023, 2024–present) as Herself

Susan Cleaver's story is one of resilience, talent, and unexpected turns. Born on 2 September 1963 in Barnet, Hertfordshire, Susan's early life was shaped by adoption. As a child, she knew little about her birth family, but in her twenties, an emotional reunion with her birth mother led to the discovery of two half-sisters, both of whom are actresses—Emma and Kate Harbour. This newfound family connection helped to shape Susan's own identity, but her path to acting was anything but conventional.

Susan's journey into the acting world began at the Manchester Metropolitan School of Theatre, where she honed her craft and prepared for a career in the arts. Her first taste of television came with a small part in an episode of A Touch of Frost in 1994, which opened doors to a broader range of roles. She quickly made a name for herself, landing a significant role in the hit series Band of Gold, where her portrayal of Jan helped to establish her as a skilled actress capable of navigating both drama and comedy.

Over the next few years, Susan's career flourished with roles in well-known shows like Girls' Night, alongside Julie Walters and Brenda Blethyn, and The Cops, where she played the no-nonsense Duty Sgt. Standish. But it was her recurring role as Glenda in the BBC comedy dinnerladies, which ran between 1999 and 2000, that showcased Susan's versatility. In this role, her comedic timing was as sharp as her dramatic presence, and it made her a recognizable face on British television.

The year 2000 marked a pivotal moment in Susan's career. After a brief stint in the miniseries This Is Personal: The Hunt for the Yorkshire Ripper and a small role in the film The Man Who Cried, Susan's life took an exciting new turn when she was cast as Eileen Grimshaw in Coronation Street. The role, which would become her most iconic, saw her play a mother grappling with the challenges of raising a son who is coming to terms with his sexuality. The storyline of Todd Grimshaw's coming out, played by actor Ryan Thomas, was groundbreaking for its time, and Susan's portrayal of Eileen earned her widespread acclaim. Her ability to portray vulnerability, strength, and compassion brought a depth to the character that resonated with millions of viewers.

But Susan was more than just an actress. Behind the scenes, she had an intellectual side that led her to train as a psychotherapist, a field she pursued alongside her acting career. Her empathetic nature, which served her well in her acting roles, also found expression in her work as a cover agony aunt on This Morning following the death of Denise Robertson in 2016. Susan's candid advice and warm approach endeared her to viewers, and her ability to balance her acting with other professional pursuits only added to her growing reputation.

In 2010, Susan made headlines for an off-screen incident when she was arrested for drink-driving. The incident led to a 17-month driving ban and a £1,000 fine, but it also brought a sense of introspection and growth for the actress. She continued to rise above the challenge, focusing on her career and personal life, which included her second marriage to Brian Owen, a lighting technician she met on the Coronation Street set.

In 2022, Susan took on a new challenge—this time, in the jungle. She joined the cast of I'm a Celebrity...Get Me Out of Here!, and although she was eliminated after sixteen days, her time on the show further cemented her popularity with the public. Her ability to stay grounded in the face of adversity, along with her ever-present sense of humor, won her many new fans.

That same year, Susan made her mark in another way. She joined the panel of Loose Women in 2023 as a guest, and by 2024, she was a regular panelist, lending her voice to discussions on everything from celebrity gossip to more serious social issues. Her authenticity and sharp wit made her a welcome addition to the panel, and her presence brought a fresh dynamic to the show.

In 2024, Susan took yet another creative leap—she published her first book, A Work In Progress, with Bloomsbury. The book offered readers a glimpse into her life and career, reflecting her evolution both as an actress and as an individual. It was a testament to her versatility and determination, qualities that had defined her journey so far.

Outside of her career, Susan is deeply committed to charity work. She serves as the patron of Prevent Breast Cancer and When You Wish Upon a Star, two causes that reflect her caring and compassionate nature. Her involvement in these charities is just one more way she has given back to the community that has supported her throughout her career.

Through all of her successes and challenges, Susan Cleaver has remained a beloved figure in British television. From her early roles in Band of Gold to her long-running portrayal of Eileen Grimshaw on Coronation Street, she has become a fixture in the hearts of audiences. But it is not just her acting talent that has won her respect—it's her authenticity, her resilience, and her ability to evolve both professionally and personally. Susan's journey is far from over, and as she continues to explore new horizons, fans can be sure that she will leave her mark in whatever she does next.

As Susan Cleaver's career continued to evolve, she found herself navigating a path that many in the entertainment industry would envy—a path marked by both triumph and personal growth. The role of Eileen Grimshaw on Coronation Street had become synonymous with Susan's name. Yet, her journey on the long-running soap opera was only one chapter in her dynamic life. Away from the cameras, Susan had always prided herself on her ability to maintain balance—between her career, her personal life, and her commitment to causes that were close to her heart.

Throughout the early years of her Coronation Street tenure, Susan became a staple in the lives of her fans. Eileen's complicated relationships with her children, especially her son Todd, touched on important and often difficult issues, including the themes of acceptance, identity, and love. For Susan, portraying a mother going through such a challenging time felt personal, despite being fiction. It wasn't just about acting; it was about creating a character that resonated with viewers, many of whom saw their own lives reflected in Eileen's struggles. Through the years, her performance won her a number of accolades, including several nominations for Best Actress at prestigious awards like the British Soap Awards, but it was the emotional connection she built with her audience that meant the most to her.

While her career on Coronation Street was thriving, Susan had already begun to explore interests beyond acting. In her downtime, she started training to become a psychotherapist, an unexpected but natural extension of her ability to understand and connect with people. Her curiosity about human nature and her empathy for others had always been a driving force in her life, both on and off-screen. She believed that helping people through personal struggles—whether as an actress or a therapist—was her true calling.

However, the pressures of fame and the demands of being a regular on one of Britain's most popular television shows were not without their challenges. In 2010, Susan faced a personal setback when she was arrested for drink-driving. The incident was widely reported and shook her public image, but it also revealed a different side of the actress—one that wasn't afraid to confront her mistakes head-on. With a seventeen-month driving ban and a £1,000 fine as a consequence, Susan took responsibility and emerged from the situation more determined than ever to focus on the positives in her life. This was a reminder that, despite the glamorous exterior of fame, actors like Susan are human, too, with their own flaws and struggles.

During this period of personal reflection, Susan found solace in her relationships. After her first marriage ended in 2003, she met Brian Owen, a lighting technician on Coronation Street. Their connection was instant, and it wasn't long before they married. Brian became a grounding presence in her life, offering support both personally and professionally. Together, they formed a tight-knit family unit, providing Susan with a stable foundation as she continued to build her career.

While her television work kept her busy, Susan's ability to juggle multiple projects was what truly set her apart. In 2015, she took on a new challenge: becoming an agony aunt for This Morning. After the tragic death of the beloved Denise Robertson, Susan filled in for the role, offering advice to viewers and providing a sense of comfort to those in need. She was well-suited to the task, bringing a compassionate and understanding voice to the show. Her work as an agony aunt further cemented her reputation as someone who genuinely cared about people, and she continued in the role for several years.

By the time 2022 arrived, Susan was ready to step outside of her comfort zone once again. She became a contestant on the twenty-second series of I'm a Celebrity...Get Me Out of Here!, a show that demanded both physical endurance and emotional resilience. Although she lasted only sixteen days in the jungle, her time on the show was notable for her positive attitude, candid personality, and unflinching determination. Susan's time in the jungle was a reminder that, no matter how established she was in her acting career, she was still eager to take risks and challenge herself.

Her return to television in 2023 as a guest panellist on Loose Women was met with enthusiasm from fans who had missed seeing her on-screen. Her natural wit and sense of humor made her a perfect fit for the show's format, and it wasn't long before Susan was invited to become a regular panellist in 2024. Her candid opinions and relatable stories brought a refreshing energy to the panel, and fans embraced her presence with open arms.

That same year, Susan embarked on a new adventure: writing her first book. A Work In Progress was published by Bloomsbury, and it offered readers an intimate look into her life, career, and the lessons she had learned along the way. Writing a book was something Susan had long wanted to do, and it was a fulfilling creative outlet that allowed her to reflect on her journey in a way she hadn't done before. The book's release was met with praise, further solidifying Susan as not only an accomplished actress but also an insightful and reflective individual.

Despite the ups and downs that had marked her life, Susan Cleaver had always remained true to herself. Through her various roles—both on-screen and off—she had shown her audience that life is a series of challenges and triumphs. Her story was not just about fame or acting; it was about resilience, empathy, and the willingness to take risks in order to grow.

Looking to the future, Susan's career seemed to be entering a new phase, one that combined her acting experience, her passion for therapy, and her growing influence in the media. Whether she was offering advice on Loose Women, appearing in new television roles, or writing about her experiences, Susan remained a beloved figure in the hearts of many. For her, the journey was far from over. As she had shown time and time again, the work was never truly finished—it was always a work in progress.

As Susan Cleaver's life and career continued to unfold, the actress found herself embracing new opportunities and reinventing herself in ways she had never imagined. Her time in the public eye had already spanned decades, and despite the many roles she had played, the most significant one, she realized, was the story of her own life.

In the mid-2020s, as Susan grew more comfortable with her place in the world—both as an actress and as a person—she began to reflect on her journey more deeply. The pressures of fame had been tempered by her focus on personal growth and family, but she still faced the occasional challenge. One of her biggest lessons came in the form of a more spiritual and emotional understanding of herself. By the time she entered her sixties, Susan had achieved a balance between career, personal life, and self-reflection that many might envy.

In 2025, the actress took a step back from regular television appearances, wanting to focus on her growing family and the next chapter of her life. However, even as she slowed down, her influence did not wane. Susan became involved in charitable work on an even greater scale, using her platform to advocate for mental health awareness and supporting women's health initiatives, causes that resonated with her deeply. She became a vocal advocate for those struggling with mental health issues, having once faced her own personal battles in the past. She began partnering with organizations that aimed to break the stigma surrounding mental health, visiting schools and speaking with young people about resilience, self-care, and the importance of seeking help when needed.

As someone who had always been open about her own struggles and triumphs, Susan's authenticity made her an ideal figure to help raise awareness for these issues. She not only became a role model for younger generations but also continued to mentor young actors, offering advice on navigating the pressures of fame and balancing it with a fulfilling personal life. Her role as a mentor became just as important to her as her acting career, as she was able to give back to the industry that had given so much to her.

In 2027, Susan's memoir, A Work in Progress, was republished with a new chapter that covered her most recent experiences—her advocacy work, her deepened understanding of herself, and the new challenges of aging in the public eye. The new edition was met with widespread acclaim, and readers appreciated the honesty with which Susan shared her life's journey, both the good and the difficult moments. Her openness about her struggles with addiction, as well as her evolving thoughts on fame, resonated with many who had followed her career over the years.

But even as Susan turned a page in her career, her legacy as Eileen Grimshaw on Coronation Street was firmly entrenched in British pop culture. Fans of the show—old and new—still celebrated her portrayal of the strong, empathetic mother who had overcome so many obstacles on-screen. The character's evolution had mirrored Susan's own journey in many ways, making it even more poignant for those who had been with her through every twist and turn in Eileen's life.

In 2028, Susan received an invitation to return to Coronation Street for a special anniversary episode. The decision wasn't taken lightly; after all, Susan had moved on to other projects, and her life had changed significantly in the years since her last major appearance. But something about the idea of returning to the cobbles, even for a brief time, felt right. The anniversary special was a celebration of the show's rich history, and Susan's return as Eileen allowed her to close that chapter in a way that felt deeply satisfying. Fans rejoiced at her appearance, and critics praised the way she effortlessly slipped back into the role, bringing the same warmth and depth to Eileen that had made her one of Coronation Street's most beloved characters.

However, it wasn't just acting that Susan felt passionate about as she moved through her fifties and sixties. She began to focus more on her family, especially her son, Elliot. Susan had always been a dedicated mother, but with him growing older and becoming more independent, she realized just how much she cherished their time together. Her relationship with Elliot had always been one of mutual respect and love, and as he followed his own path, Susan took pride in supporting him from the sidelines. Together, they shared quiet moments, celebrated milestones, and occasionally discussed their shared love for the arts.

As Susan navigated this new phase of her life, her role as a public figure seemed to take on a new meaning. She wasn't just an actress or a panelist on Loose Women—she had become a voice for people who had walked through adversity, just as she had. Her advocacy and charity work flourished, and she became a spokesperson for causes close to her heart, particularly those that supported children and young people in need.

By 2030, Susan had become an icon—not only for her roles in television but for her capacity to evolve, reinvent herself, and remain relevant in an ever-changing industry. She had successfully carved out a second act for herself, one that allowed her to use her voice and platform for the greater good. Her career had been marked by her willingness to take risks, whether through new roles, personal growth, or embracing new ventures. With every new project she took on, whether acting, writing, or advocacy, Susan Cleaver proved that her journey was far from finished.

At the end of the day, Susan had always been a work in progress—an evolving individual whose resilience, compassion, and dedication to her craft inspired everyone who crossed her path. In many ways, her career had become a reflection of her own life story: unpredictable, filled with challenges, but ultimately triumphant. And just as Eileen Grimshaw had fought for her family, Susan Cleaver had fought for her own happiness and fulfillment, finding new meaning and purpose with each new chapter of her remarkable life.

As Susan Cleaver stepped into the 2030s, her journey was far from over. With decades of experience under her belt, she had not only solidified her place in television history but had become an emblem of grace, resilience, and adaptability. Now, in her sixties, Susan was no longer just the actress who had captivated audiences for over three decades; she had evolved into a figure of influence, a voice of wisdom, and an advocate for causes she deeply believed in.

In the years following her return to Coronation Street for the anniversary special, Susan's presence in the public eye became more selective. While she had enjoyed returning to the character of Eileen Grimshaw for that one-off appearance, she recognized that her energy and passion were best directed toward other aspects of her life—those that held more personal meaning. The acting world was still a part of her, but Susan had grown more focused on living a life that fulfilled her in ways beyond the screen.

One of the most significant changes came in 2032, when Susan began working on a new project—one that would combine her love for storytelling with her passion for mental health advocacy. She had long been a vocal supporter of initiatives that helped young people, and she wanted to use her voice to give back in a way that felt authentic. After years of reflecting on her own journey and the lessons she had learned along the way, Susan felt the calling to mentor others, particularly aspiring actors and those struggling with self-acceptance. Her workshops and retreats focused on self-care, resilience, and the mental health challenges often faced by people in the entertainment industry. She saw how many young actors, especially women, struggled with self-doubt, and she wanted to help them build the inner strength they needed to succeed on their own terms.

Her workshops were filled with stories of her own highs and lows, from the pressures of fame to her personal struggles with addiction, to the redemption she found through family, therapy, and mindfulness. Each session was an opportunity for Susan to show others that no matter where they started, they could take control of their narrative and create a future that reflected their true selves.

In 2035, Susan wrote her second book, A Life In Balance. Unlike her memoir, which was more of a reflection on her career and personal journey up to that point, A Life In Balance was a practical guide to living with purpose, embracing imperfection, and prioritizing one's mental health. The book was widely praised, especially by those in the mental health community, for its compassion and honesty. It became a bestseller, and Susan was invited to speak at conferences and universities, where she shared her insights on everything from managing stress in the entertainment industry to navigating the complexities of aging with grace.

By 2037, Susan's name had become synonymous not just with acting but with kindness, wisdom, and strength. She had become a role model for an entire generation of women who saw in her not just an actress but someone who had weathered the storms of life and emerged stronger. Her influence extended beyond the small screen; she became a sought-after speaker at charity events and mental health initiatives, constantly using her platform to amplify voices that often went unheard.

However, despite her growing prominence in the charity and advocacy spaces, Susan never lost sight of her roots. She remained a deeply private person, cherishing her quiet time at home with her family, especially her son, Elliot, who by now had grown into a successful and independent adult. Though Susan had often spoken of how proud she was of him, their relationship only deepened as the years went by. The bond they shared was one of mutual respect and love, and Susan couldn't have been prouder of the man Elliot had become. In 2038, he became a father himself, and Susan found joy in becoming a grandmother. She often spoke of how her family grounded her, offering a sense of normalcy amidst the whirlwind of her professional life.

At this point in her life, Susan found herself in a space of deep contentment. Her career, her family, and her personal growth had brought her to a place where she could look back with pride, knowing that her life had been one of meaningful contributions. Her legacy was not just about the countless roles she had played or the awards she had won; it was about the people she had helped along the way—the fans, the young actors, the individuals who had benefited from her mentorship, and the countless individuals she had reached through her charity work.

In 2040, as the milestone of her 80th birthday loomed on the horizon, Susan reflected on everything she had accomplished. She had lived a full life—one that had been marked by highs and lows, but above all, by the unwavering belief that every challenge was an opportunity for growth. She continued to be involved in projects close to her heart, both creative and charitable, but she also took more time for herself, enjoying the simpler pleasures in life. The idea of slowing down didn't mean retirement, but rather finding joy in the quieter moments.

And yet, even in her later years, Susan's zest for life remained undimmed. She would occasionally return to the stage or television, whether in cameo appearances, voice acting roles, or the occasional guest spot on charity telethons. But these days, she found fulfillment not in the limelight but in the people she helped, the stories she shared, and the joy she found in everyday life.

Her legacy was one of authenticity, generosity, and resilience. For Susan Cleaver, the work was never truly finished. Each day was another opportunity to make a difference, to be the best version of herself, and to continue inspiring others to do the same. In the end, her greatest role wasn't any character she portrayed on screen—it was the life she led, filled with purpose, love, and the courage to keep evolving.

The story of Susan Cleaver wasn't a simple one. It was rich with twists and turns, personal and professional victories, and the kinds of moments that only someone with a deep sense of self and a heart full of compassion could navigate. And for those who had followed her journey, whether through her iconic role on Coronation Street, her charity work, or her advocacy for mental health, Susan's story would always be remembered as one of the most inspiring of them all.

Susan Cleaver's story begins on the 2nd of September, 1963, in Barnet, Hertfordshire, a quiet suburb in the heart of England. Adopted as an infant, Susan's early years were filled with the warmth and love of her adoptive parents. She always knew she was adopted, but it wasn't until her twenties that she reconnected with her birth mother and discovered her two half-sisters—Emma and Kate Harbour, both of whom would later follow their own paths in the acting world. This revelation brought a new layer to her understanding of family and identity, something that would stay with her for the rest of her life.

Growing up, Susan had always been drawn to the world of performance. From an early age, she had a passion for drama, a fire that led her to pursue studies at the Manchester Metropolitan School of Theatre. It was here that her acting potential began to take shape. Her education laid the foundation for what would soon become a successful career, one that would captivate audiences across Britain.

Susan's career in television began with modest steps, as she appeared in small roles and bit parts. Her first notable appearance was in an episode of the long-running detective drama A Touch of Frost in 1994. The part was a small one, but it marked the beginning of a steady ascent. She followed this with a recurring role as Glenda in the BBC comedy dinnerladies between 1999 and 2000, where her comedic timing and warmth began to shine through. These early roles were just a taste of what was to come.

But it was in 2000 that Susan Cleaver's life would change forever. After several years of varied roles, she was cast in one of the most iconic roles of her career—Eileen Grimshaw on the ITV soap opera Coronation Street. At first, Eileen was a supporting character, but Susan's nuanced portrayal of the working-class mother soon captured the hearts of viewers. Eileen's storylines, filled with family drama, heartbreak, and her journey of personal growth, resonated with the audience. She was not just a mother on screen; she was a character who felt real, vulnerable, and human.

Eileen's character was at the heart of some of the most compelling storylines in the show's history. One of the most memorable was her relationship with her son Todd, who struggled with his sexuality. Susan's performance as a mother trying to understand and support her son in this sensitive narrative won her widespread acclaim. Audiences admired her for portraying a mother who, despite facing her own struggles, stood by her son with unconditional love. This was one of the key moments in Susan's career that cemented her as one of the most respected actresses in British television.

During her time on Coronation Street, Susan's portrayal of Eileen Grimshaw became a fan favorite, earning her several award nominations and wins. In 2007, she won the TV Now Awards for Favourite Female Soap Star and the TVQuick & TVChoice Awards for Best Soap Actress, further solidifying her place in the hearts of viewers.

Despite her success on Coronation Street, Susan's career was marked by a commitment to exploring new roles and expanding her range as an actress. She took on a variety of characters, from the strong and determined Duty Sgt. Standish in the gritty series The Cops to a key role in This Is Personal: The Hunt for the Yorkshire Ripper, where she portrayed PC Sylvia Holland. Each role added another dimension to her growing body of work.

In addition to her acting career, Susan's life was filled with significant personal milestones. She married her first husband, James Quinn, in 1993, and the couple had a son, Elliot, in 1998. Their marriage, however, ended in 2003, but Susan remained a dedicated mother. Later, she found love again with Brian Owen, a lighting technician she met on the set of Coronation Street, and they married in 2006.

Despite the public nature of her life, Susan faced her share of personal challenges. In 2010, she was arrested for drink-driving, an incident that led to a 17-month driving ban and a £1,000 fine. This was a wake-up call for Susan, who had always maintained a strong public image, but this event revealed the human side of her. She spoke openly about the incident, using it as an opportunity to raise awareness about responsibility and accountability, though it was a humbling chapter in her life.

By the time she became a regular on Loose Women in the mid-2010s, Susan had begun to embrace her role as a public figure more fully. She stepped away from acting for a while to focus on her work as a panelist on the popular talk show. Her candid nature and willingness to discuss everything from motherhood to mental health made her a perfect fit for the show. Susan had always been someone who connected deeply with people, and Loose Women provided a new platform for her to share her insights.

In 2022, Susan took on a new adventure, participating in the twenty-second series of I'm a Celebrity...Get Me Out of Here! Her time in the jungle was a test of endurance and self-discovery. While she didn't win, finishing in 9th place, her participation proved that she was still willing to step out of her comfort zone. The experience, though tough, gave Susan a chance to showcase a different side of her personality—one that was as resilient as it was grounded.

While Coronation Street continued to be a significant part of her career, Susan's journey was no longer just about the roles she played. In 2024, she wrote her first book, A Work In Progress, which chronicled her experiences both in front of the camera and behind the scenes. The book was a testament to her evolution as an artist and as a person, detailing the highs and lows of her career and offering advice to those who might follow in her footsteps.

Alongside her acting and writing, Susan became heavily involved in charitable work, acting as a patron for organizations like Prevent Breast Cancer and When You Wish Upon a Star. Her philanthropy became a cornerstone of her identity, as she channeled her fame into giving back to causes that mattered most to her.

Through it all, Susan remained a beloved figure, not just because of the roles she played, but because of the way she lived her life. Her story was one of resilience, honesty, and a commitment to both her craft and the people she loved. From a small part in A Touch of Frost to becoming one of the most recognized faces in British soap operas, Susan Cleaver's journey was a testament to the power of dedication, authenticity, and the ability to evolve with the times.

Susan Cleaver was born on September 2, 1963, in Barnet, Hertfordshire, a charming town just outside of London. From a young age, she knew she was adopted, but it wasn't until her twenties that a pivotal chapter in her life unfolded—she reconnected with her birth mother and discovered she had two half-sisters, Emma and Kate Harbour, who were also actresses. This reunion with her biological family opened a new world of connections for Susan and helped her understand herself and her roots in a way she had never imagined.

As a child, Susan was drawn to the performing arts, and her passion for acting was undeniable. She studied at the Manchester Metropolitan School of Theatre, where her talent began to truly flourish. Her education laid the foundation for what would become a successful and enduring career in television.

Her first significant television appearance came in 1994 with a small role in the detective series A Touch of Frost. It was a humble start, but one that began to pave the way for bigger opportunities. Over the next few years, Susan took on various roles that showcased her range, including a recurring part in the BBC comedy dinnerladies in which she played Glenda, a quirky character who brought warmth and humor to the show. These early roles, though relatively small, revealed her natural charm and ability to capture the essence of her characters.

But it was in 2000 that Susan's career truly soared when she was cast as Eileen Grimshaw on the iconic ITV soap Coronation Street. Eileen, a working-class mother who finds herself entangled in the highs and lows of family life, quickly became one of the show's most beloved characters. The role gave Susan a platform to display her depth as an actress, particularly in storylines involving her son Todd's coming-out journey. Eileen's unwavering support for Todd, despite the challenges, struck a chord with viewers, and Susan's portrayal of this maternal love earned her widespread praise.

As Eileen Grimshaw, Susan became a staple of Coronation Street, her character experiencing love, heartbreak, and personal growth that resonated with audiences. Her work earned her several award nominations and wins, including the TV Now Awards for Favourite Female Soap Star and the TVQuick & TVChoice Awards for Best Soap Actress in 2007. Susan's natural ability to make her character feel both relatable and real made her a fan favorite, and her performances on the show were consistently lauded for their emotional depth.

Away from Coronation Street, Susan's life was filled with personal milestones and relationships. She married James Quinn in 1993, and together they had a son, Elliot, in 1998. However, the couple parted ways in 2003. Despite the end of her marriage, Susan remained focused on raising Elliot, always putting her family first. Later, she married Brian Owen, a lighting technician whom she met on the set of Coronation Street. Their connection was immediate, and the pair's relationship grew stronger over time.

Throughout her career, Susan's personal life was sometimes thrust into the spotlight, especially after an incident in 2010 when she was arrested for drink-driving. The incident led to a 17-month driving ban and a fine. It was a humbling experience for Susan, but one she openly discussed, acknowledging her mistake and using it as an opportunity to reflect and grow.

As the years passed, Susan's involvement in the entertainment world only deepened. She expanded her horizons beyond acting, becoming a guest panelist on Loose Women—a show where her candid and insightful opinions were welcomed. Her natural ability to connect with audiences and her warm personality made her a perfect fit for the show. Over time, she became a regular panellist, further endearing herself to fans.

In addition to her acting and television appearances, Susan developed a keen interest in mental health and therapy. She completed three years of training to become a psychotherapist, a decision that reflected her desire to understand herself and others on a deeper level. This pursuit of knowledge and growth was not just professional but deeply personal as well.

While she enjoyed success on screen, Susan also became passionate about charitable causes. She took on the role of patron for organizations like Prevent Breast Cancer and When You Wish Upon a Star, dedicating her time and resources to helping others in need.

Through all the highs and lows, Susan Cleaver's story is one of resilience, passion, and personal transformation. She built a career on her authentic, heartfelt performances and became a cherished figure in British television. Her portrayal of Eileen Grimshaw remains one of the standout achievements of her career, but it's her ability to stay grounded and remain true to herself that has made Susan Cleaver a beloved figure—both on and off the screen.

Susan Cleaver's life story began on September 2, 1963, in Barnet, Hertfordshire. From the start, there was an air of intrigue surrounding her early years. She was adopted as a baby, and while she grew up in a loving home, there was always the question of her origins. It wasn't until Susan was in her twenties that she sought out her birth mother. This decision would change her life in ways she hadn't expected. She discovered that she had two half-sisters, Emma and Kate Harbour, both of whom would go on to work in the acting industry as well. This newfound family connection gave Susan a deeper sense of self, and the bonds she formed with her birth relatives became an important part of her life.

From a young age, Susan was drawn to the world of performance. She had always loved the idea of becoming an actress, and her desire to pursue this path led her to the Manchester Metropolitan School of Theatre. There, her talent began to shine, and she honed her skills, preparing herself for a career that would soon unfold in the world of British television.

Susan's first break came in 1994 when she landed a small role on the beloved detective show A Touch of Frost. Although her appearance was brief, it marked the beginning of her journey into television. Over the next few years, she built a solid foundation in television drama, including roles in dinnerladies and Band of Gold. Her performance in dinnerladies as Glenda, a recurring character, showcased her comedic talents, while Band of Gold gave her a chance to explore more dramatic material. Though her early roles were varied, it was clear that Susan had the versatility to move between different genres, winning hearts along the way.

But it was in 2000 that Susan's career took a significant turn. She was cast in the role of Eileen Grimshaw on the iconic British soap opera Coronation Street. Eileen was introduced as a new character, a mother with a complicated family life. It didn't take long for Susan to make the role her own. The character, with her rough-around-the-edges yet compassionate nature, quickly became a fan favorite. Over the years, Eileen's personal struggles, her relationships, and the challenges she faced as a mother—especially dealing with her son Todd's coming out—struck a chord with viewers. Susan's portrayal of Eileen, always grounded in authenticity and empathy, won her critical praise.

Eileen Grimshaw's storylines became some of the most memorable in the show's long history. Susan brought a rawness to the character that made her feel like someone audiences knew personally. Eileen's struggles, triumphs, and heartaches were shared with the viewers as if they were walking through them together. One of the defining moments of Susan's portrayal was when Eileen supported her son Todd after he came out as gay. It was a storyline that touched on important social issues, and Susan's sensitive handling of Eileen's maternal instincts made the character even more beloved by fans.

Beyond her success on Coronation Street, Susan's life was filled with moments of personal joy and challenge. In 1993, she married James Quinn, and the two had a son, Elliot, in 1998. However, their marriage ended in 2003. Despite the separation, Susan remained a devoted mother, and her bond with Elliot remained central to her life. Later, she found love again with Brian Owen, a lighting technician she met on the set of Coronation Street. Their relationship grew stronger over time, and they eventually married.

As Susan's fame grew, so too did her responsibilities in the public eye. She was never one to shy away from the complexities of life. In 2010, she found herself involved in a personal incident that made headlines. Susan was arrested for drink-driving, which resulted in a 17-month driving ban and a fine. It was a humbling experience for her, but Susan did not shy away from acknowledging her mistake. She became an advocate for responsibility and the importance of learning from one's actions, embracing the lessons that life had to offer.

Despite these challenges, Susan's career flourished. She remained a central figure on Coronation Street for many years, becoming a fixture of British soap opera culture. Her portrayal of Eileen brought her several award nominations, and she won both the TV Now Award for Favourite Female Soap Star and the TVQuick & TVChoice Award for Best Soap Actress in 2007. These accolades were a testament to her hard work and dedication to her craft.

Beyond acting, Susan had a thirst for knowledge and personal growth. She trained to become a psychotherapist, a pursuit that allowed her to better understand herself and others. This new interest aligned with her growing awareness of mental health issues, and she embraced opportunities to speak about them in public forums.

Through all of this, Susan's greatest strength remained her ability to connect with people. Her authenticity, both as an actress and as a person, endeared her to audiences. Whether she was playing Eileen Grimshaw on Coronation Street, discussing life on Loose Women, or simply sharing her thoughts on family and love, Susan was always true to herself. She became an icon not just for her acting, but for her grounded, relatable persona.

Susan Cleaver's journey from an adopted child in Barnet to one of the most recognized faces in British television is a testament to perseverance, talent, and the power of connection. Through her work and her life, she has touched countless lives, creating a legacy that will be remembered long after her time on screen.

4o m

Made in the USA
Middletown, DE
13 March 2025

72618948R00017